Daily dash diary

WRITING JOURNAL

Topics to write about

Name:

What I am most interested in doing in all the world is ...

I think it's wrong when people ...

If I could talk to anyone in the world it would be ...

Graeme Beals

Written by Graeme Beals © Curriculum Concepts 1999
Revised and republished by R.I.C. Publications® 2000, 2001, 2007, 2012

 **R.I.C. Publications®**

 **Prim-Ed** Publishing

I wrote my DAILY DASHES in the following order:

Date   **Title**

/ _____

/ _____

/ _____

/ _____

/ _____

/ _____

/ _____

/ _____

/ _____

/ _____

/ _____

/ _____

/ _____

/ _____

/ _____

/ _____

/ _____

/ _____

/ _____

/ _____

/ _____

/ _____

/ _____

/ _____

/ _____

I wrote my DAILY DASHES in the following order:

Date	Title
/	_____
/	_____
/	_____
/	_____
/	_____
/	_____
/	_____
/	_____
/	_____
/	_____
/	_____
/	_____
/	_____
/	_____
/	_____
/	_____
/	_____
/	_____
/	_____
/	_____
/	_____
/	_____
/	_____
/	_____
/	_____

Before you start ...

Think carefully about what is important to you.

★ Decide how you feel or felt about the topic.

★ Jot down keywords.

★ Think about main ideas/paragraphs.

★ Think of sentences in your mind before writing.

When you've finished, check ...

✔ Paragraphs

✔ Punctuation

✔ Spelling

✔ Use of adjectives

✔ Does it make sense?

www.ricpublications.com.au – R.I.C. Publications®

My favourite TV show is ...

What do I like about it?

The KINDEST person I know is …

What makes this person kind?

The funniest thing I ever saw was ...
Why was it so funny?

The piece of **clothing**
I like best of all is my ...
What makes it my favourite?

_____

_____

_____

_____

_____

_____

_____

_____

_____

_____

_____

_____

_____

_____

_____

_____

_____

_____

_____

_____

_____

_____

www.ricpublications.com.au – R.I.C. Publications®

My favourite food is ...

Why is it my favourite? When do I like to eat it?

One day
I would like
to ...

Why would I like to do this?

_____

_____

_____

_____

_____

_____

_____

_____

_____

_____

_____

_____

_____

_____

_____

_____

_____

_____

_____

_____

_____

_____

_____

_____

_____

www.ricpublications.com.au – R.I.C. Publications®

The best I've ever done in sport is ...

The nicest thing I ever did for anyone was ...

Choice

_____

_____

_____

_____

_____

_____

_____

_____

_____

_____

_____

_____

_____

_____

_____

_____

_____

_____

_____

_____

_____

_____

_____

_____

_____

_____

_____

_____

_____

The most beautiful things in the world are ...

www.ricpublications.com.au – R.I.C. Publications®

My favourite pet is ...

Why do I like it?

_____

_____

_____

_____

_____

_____

_____

_____

_____

_____

_____

_____

_____

_____

_____

_____

_____

_____

_____

_____

_____

_____

_____

_____

_____

_____

What was
GOOD
about it?

www.ricpublications.com.au – R.I.C. Publications®

The thing I hate doing most in the world is ...

How does it make me feel?

Why do I hate it?

_____

_____

_____

_____

_____

_____

_____

_____

_____

_____

_____

_____

_____

_____

_____

_____

_____

_____

_____

_____

_____

_____

_____

_____

The advertisement I like the most on TV is ...

_____

_____

_____

_____

_____

_____

_____

_____

_____

_____

_____

_____

_____

_____

_____

_____

_____

_____

_____

_____

_____

_____

_____

_____

When I am ANGRY,
I...

What I am most interested in doing in all the world is ...

_____

_____

_____

_____

_____

_____

_____

_____

_____

_____

_____

_____

_____

_____

_____

_____

_____

_____

_____

_____

_____

_____

_____

_____

_____

_____

_____

_____

_____

_____

_____

Why do I want to do this?

The cleverest thing I ever did was ...

What happened as a result of it?

If I won a million dollars, I would ...

An old person once told me ...

www.ricpublications.com.au – R.I.C. Publications®

How did it make me feel?

The **worst** dream I ever had was ...

I feel PROUD of myself when ...

Why am I so proud?

Sometimes I feel shy when ...

What makes me shy?

What I'd really like to be able to do is ...

Why do I want to be able to do this?

A peaceful place I like to go is …

Why do I like to go there?

The cleverest person I know is ...
Why is this person so clever?

www.ricpublications.com.au – R.I.C. Publications®

If I could buy one person any gift, I'd buy ...

Who would I buy it for?

Why would I buy it?

_____

_____

_____

_____

_____

_____

_____

_____

_____

_____

_____

_____

_____

_____

_____

_____

_____

_____

_____

_____

_____

_____

_____

_____

_____

The advertisement
I hate the most on TV is ...

What do I hate about it?

Choice
Choice
Choice
Choice
Choice
Choice
Choice
Choice
Choice
Choice

My favourite sport is …

Why do I like this sport?

I remember feeling **sad** when ...

Why did it make me sad?

If I could change one thing in the world, I'd change …

WHY WOULD I CHANGE IT?

The worst pain I ever felt was when ...

The best meal I ever had was ...

_____
_____
_____
_____
_____
_____
_____
_____
_____
_____
_____
_____
_____
_____
_____
_____
_____
_____
_____
_____
_____
_____
_____
_____
_____

www.ricpublications.com.au – R.I.C. Publications®

The first thing I remember is ...

Memory

FRIGHTENED

I am very frightened when ...

Why does it frighten me?

THE TALENTS I HAVE ARE ...

Friends are important to me because ...

www.ricpublications.com.au – R.I.C. Publications®

One thing I'd really like to know is …
Why would I like to know this?

My favourite memory is ...

Why is it my favourite?

SOMEONE I WOULD REALLY LIKE TO HELP IS ...

Why would I like to help this person?

What would I like to do?

www.ricpublications.com.au – R.I.C. Publications®

Something I learnt recently is ...

Sometimes I feel

FRUSTRATED

when . . .

Why do I feel
frustrated?

_____

_____

_____

_____

_____

_____

_____

_____

_____

_____

_____

_____

_____

_____

_____

_____

_____

_____

_____

_____

_____

_____

_____

_____

_____

_____

_____

www.ricpublications.com.au – R.I.C. Publications®

My favourite singer is ...

Why do I like this singer?

The **hardest thing**
I ever had to do was ...

Sometimes I wonder ...

Choice

Something I hope NEVER happens is ...

Something I'm not good at
and need to improve is ...

How can I improve it?

My favourite thing I own is ...

Why is it my favourite?

I think it's wrong
when people …

Why do I think
it is wrong?

The most bored
I have ever been
was ...

Why was I so bored?

I wish someone would help me...

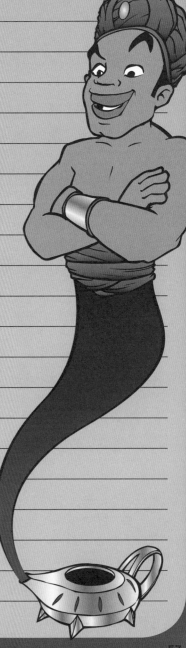

Why do you want help with this?

I felt really MEAN
one day when ...

Something
I will never forget is ...

One thing I truly believe, but some other people don't, is ...

_____
_____
_____
_____
_____
_____
_____
_____
_____
_____
_____
_____
_____
_____
_____
_____
_____
_____
_____
_____
_____
_____
_____
_____
_____

I think the important things in life are ...

I feel HAPPIEST
in the world when ...

Why does this make me happy?

Something I am embarrassed about is ...

Why am I embarrassed about it?

HIC!

If I could,
I would like to design a . . .

The person I trust the most is...

Why do I trust this person?

_____

_____

_____

_____

_____

_____

_____

_____

_____

_____

_____

_____

_____

_____

_____

_____

_____

_____

_____

_____

_____

_____

_____

www.ricpublications.com.au – R.I.C. Publications®

When I'm Older I Would like to...

_____

_____

_____

_____

_____

_____

_____

_____

_____

_____

_____

_____

_____

_____

_____

_____

_____

_____

_____

_____

_____

_____

_____

_____

_____

_____

_____

_____

If I could go on a trip, I would like to visit...
Why do I want to go to this place?

_____
_____
_____
_____
_____
_____
_____
_____
_____
_____
_____
_____
_____
_____
_____
_____
_____
_____
_____
_____
_____
_____
_____

My Favourite part of the day is ...

If I had special powers I would like to be able to ...

Why do I want to be able to do this?

www.ricpublications.com.au – R.I.C. Publications®

Choice Choice Choice Choice Choice Choice Choice Choice Choice Choice Choice

The country I would most like to visit is ...

Why would I like to visit this country?

_____
_____
_____
_____
_____
_____
_____
_____
_____
_____
_____
_____
_____
_____
_____
_____
_____
_____
_____
_____
_____
_____

www.ricpublications.com.au – R.I.C. Publications®

The best joke I've ever heard is ...

THE SUBJECT I MOST LIKE AT SCHOOL IS ...

What do I like about this subject?

_____

_____

_____

_____

_____

_____

_____

_____

_____

_____

_____

_____

_____

_____

_____

_____

_____

_____

_____

_____

_____

_____

_____

_____

_____

_____

The subject I least like at school is ...

What don't I like about this subject?

I make a good friend because ...

I would like to meet ...

Why do I want to meet this person?

_____

_____

_____

_____

_____

_____

_____

_____

_____

_____

_____

_____

_____

_____

_____

_____

_____

_____

_____

_____

_____

_____

_____

_____

_____

Autographs

If I could time travel, I would go ...
Why do I want to go there?

www.ricpublications.com.au – R.I.C. Publications®

I wish I had NEVER ...

Why do I wish I'd never done this?

_____

_____

_____

_____

_____

_____

_____

_____

_____

_____

_____

_____

_____

_____

_____

_____

_____

_____

_____

_____

_____

_____

I'd like to be famous for ...

Choice

IF I COULD BE AN ANIMAL, I WOULD BE ...

Why did I choose this animal?

THE MOST FUN I'VE EVER HAD WAS WHEN ...

_____
_____
_____
_____
_____
_____
_____
_____
_____
_____
_____
_____
_____
_____
_____
_____
_____
_____
_____
_____
_____
_____
_____
_____
_____
_____
_____

If I could talk to anyone in the world it would be ... and I would ask ...

The top 10 things about me are ...

1. _____

_____

2. _____

_____

3. _____

_____

4. _____

_____

5. _____

_____

6. _____

_____

7. _____

_____

8. _____

_____

9. _____

_____

10. _____

_____

The things I would most like people to know about me are ...

The planet I would most like to visit is ...

Why would I like to go there?

The thing I am best at in all the world is ...

What I like doing best on my birthday is . . .

Why do I like doing this on my birthday?

To relax, I like to ...

www.ricpublications.com.au – R.I.C. Publications®

Choice
Choice
Choice
Choice
Choice
Choice
Choice
Choice
Choice

My favourite TV character is ...

What do I like about this character?

www.ricpublications.com.au – R.I.C. Publications®

Some Extra Ideas

The nicest flavour of all is ...

What I like best about my bed is ...

One food I'll never eat is ...

I choose a book by ...

The worst smell I have ever smelt is ...

To make my favourite meal, I have to ...

The best cook in my family is ...

The weekend is ...

I like to laugh because ...

My favourite season of the year is ...

The song I most like to listen to is ...

My favourite colour is ...

My favourite room at home is ...

Autographs